HOW WOULD YOU VOTE
IF YOU WERE ALLOWED TO?

Experience the Power of
Direct Democracy and
Make Your Voice Heard

W.R. WILKERSON III

Copyright © 2006 Wilkerson Family Partnership, FLP

All rights reserved. Without limiting the rights under copyright reserved above, no part of this publication may be reproduced, stored in, or introduced into a retrieval system, or transmitted, in any form or by any means (electronic, mechanical, photocopying, recording, or otherwise), without the prior written permission of both the copyright owner and the above publisher of this book, except in the case of brief quotations embodied in critical reviews and certain other noncommercial uses permitted by copyright law. For permission requests, write to the publisher, addressed "Attention: Permissions Coordinator," at the address below.

Ciro's Books, Inc.
18627 Brookhurst Street, #350
Fountain Valley, CA 92708
Tel: (714) 849-6333   www.cirosbooks.com

Ordering Information

Quantity sales. Special discounts are available on quantity purchases by corporations, associations, and others. For details, contact the "Special Sales Department" at the Ciro's Books address above.

Individual sales. Ciro's Books publications are available through most bookstores. They can also be ordered directly from Ciro's Books.

Orders for college textbook/course adoption use. Please contact Ciro's Books.

Orders by U.S. trade bookstores and wholesalers. Please contact Ciro's Books.

Printed in the United States of America

Cataloging-in-Publication Data
Wilkerson, W. R., 1951-
   How would you vote if you were allowed to? : experience the power of direct democracy and make your voice heard / W. R. Wilkerson, III.
   p. cm.
   Includes index.
   ISBN 0-9676643-3-0
1. Direct democracy—United States. 2. Democracy—United States—Citizen participation. 3. Elections—United States—Citizen participation.
4. Referendum—United States. 5. Political participation—United States.
6. United States—Politics and government. I. Title.
JF494.W55   2006
328.273 22—dc22   2006903047

FIRST EDITION
11 10 09 08 07 06   10 9 8 7 6 5 4 3 2 1

Cover design by Catherine Lau Hunt.
Interior design by Beverly Butterfield, Girl of the West Productions.
Copyediting by PeopleSpeak.
Index by Rachel Rice.

*For Thomas Paine,
author of the American Revolution,
and for my son, Will, who gave me
the idea of direct democracy*

Contents

Preface vii

Introduction: Where We Are—Direct Democracy Defined 1

Abortion 7

Affirmative Action 9

Alcohol & Tobacco Prohibition 11

Amending the Constitution 13

Capital Punishment 15

Electoral College 17

Entitlements (Social Security & Welfare) 19

Foreign Aid 21

Foster Care 23

Free Speech 25

Gambling 27

Gun Banning 29

Illegal Immigration 31

Mandatory National Service 33

Medicaid 35

Military Spending 37

Narcotics Decriminalization 39

National Debt 41

National Identity Card 43

National Language 45

Pornography 47

Prostitution 49

Public School Financing 51

Separation of Church & State 53

Taxation 55
Terrorism & Antiterrorist Measures 57
Universal Healthcare 59
Voluntary Euthanasia 61
Take Action! 62
Voter Ballot 63
Appendices
    Razor Thin Victories and Other Close Election Calls 65
    The Constitution of the United States 71
    Amendments to the Constitution of the United States 87
    The Declaration of Independence 99
Notes 105
Index 109
About the Author 111

Preface

I wrote this book for two reasons. The first is because of my frustration over the presidential election of 2000. In my opinion, it was in fact a decision, not an election. Our vote was hijacked by the Supreme Court, which made a decision for us. In truth, no Supreme Court, or any court for that matter, should interfere with a presidential election. I contend that given the option, Americans would have been delighted to revote on such an important issue rather than letting a court decide the matter.

But the real question for me is, where has all the fairness gone in our country? Is it right for courts to override the will and wishes of millions of Americans? Is this really democracy? I find it ironic that the very democracy we export—free and open elections in Iraq, for example—is the very democracy we fail to practice here.

The second reason I wrote this book is because our youth are gripped by a terrible wave of apathy concerning voting. I have a son in his early twenties who does not vote. When I ask him why he doesn't, his reply is always the same: "My vote doesn't count." And to a great degree, he is right. America's youth are staying away from the polls because they look around and see that key decisions are being made by the few, rather than by the millions. To them, voters are discounted when millions vote and a few overturn the voters' decision later.

W. R. Wilkerson III
April 2006

Introduction: Where We Are— Direct Democracy Defined

Democracy is America's most precious possession. So why is it that so many Americans feel disenfranchised and disconnected from their government? The answer is simple. Many Americans feel that our political and governmental system does not work for them. Most importantly, they feel that it does not hear their voice. As a result, many people don't even bother to vote because they believe their votes don't count. People have gone to the polls, cast ballots on issues they felt passionate about, and celebrated when their measure "won" only to see it overturned later by a single judge who was appointed, not voted, into office.

We pride ourselves that our system of government is based on fairness. But is it fair that a single judge can strike down a measure that millions have voted on? In 1994, for instance, 59 percent of the voters in California cast their ballots in favor of Proposition 187, a controversial measure to deny health benefits and education to illegal immigrants. On March 19, 1998, the measure was struck down by a single federal judge, Mariana Pfaelzer, thus denying the voters their prerogative. Clearly, fairness is something that cannot be determined by the courts or the government but only by the people.

The awful truth is that the people do not decide the outcome of many elections. The courts do. People don't make the key decisions that affect their lives. The courts do. Should the Supreme Court, or any court, be able to overrule the will and wishes of millions of Americans? That's a very good question. Lest we forget, nine judges, not the people of this country, decided the presidential election of 2000, when, in one of the closest elections in U.S. history, George W. Bush was declared the winner by a Supreme Court decision that ended the debate about 527 Florida votes that were to determine the state's 25 electoral votes. What does it tell us when the presidency of the United States is decided not by voters but by a court? And what good does the will of the people do if our government and judges have the ability to overturn our votes and decisions?

Let's take a moment to briefly review how our system of government works and consider whether the system in place works for us. We vote for politicians who represent us. We give them "power of attorney" so that they can act on our behalf. They, in turn, pass legislation that becomes law in matters that affect our lives and well-being. Yet once the original voting into office is over, how many of us really feel we are consulted or included in this vital decision-making process? Once politicians are voted in, the voters who got them there are excluded from the legislative process. The majority vote does not necessarily become law.

We live in a bureaucracy, not a democracy. We live in a country ruled not by its people but by its politicians. Any government body that makes decisions on behalf of its people is essentially the ruling body. Two hundred ninety-eight million Americans are ruled by 9 Supreme Court justices, 100 senators, and 435 congressional representatives.[1] Politicians have ruled over us for more than two centuries. At issue is whether our government is functioning in our best interests.

Even politicians are often excluded from direct action because much in Washington is determined by committees and subcommittees. Committees and hearings are created for just about everything, all at great taxpayer expense. The way politics functions in our country is that problems are left alone until they become crises. When Hurricane Katrina devastated the population of New Orleans and surrounding areas, it became painfully clear that the Federal Emergency Management Agency (FEMA) was not functioning the way it needed to function. The Army Corps of Engineers had been asking for money for at least a decade to shore up the levee system surrounding New Orleans, which failed and resulted in uncontrolled flooding. By most estimates, rebuilding that city will cost taxpayers more than $200 billion. The Army Corps of Engineers was asking for $27 million.[2]

But what if we took that power back and made decisions for ourselves? What would our country be like? What would our lives be like?

THE POWER OF DIRECT DEMOCRACY

Many of our current issues—guns, healthcare, abortion—could be decided with a national vote. American citizens would identify the issues and then put them to a vote. Citizens would go to the polls and register their preferences. The ballot items with a majority vote would immediately become law and would remain law for ten years. It's that simple. This system would put an end to all the nonstop debating and bickering that often paralyzes our lawmakers. It would make voting citizens both the decision makers and the lawmakers. Once the people had spoken, their say would be final. This political system is called direct democracy. Congress can still debate and work out the details of issues like highway funding, but hot topics that need clarification—school prayer, medical marijuana, and abortion, to name a few—should be put to a citizens' vote.

In a direct democracy, the power belongs not to the politicians but to the people. After an election, no court or legal challenge of any kind is allowed. No single judge or group of judges can rule a vote unconstitutional. People can protest all they want, but once the votes are tallied, the decision is final and we must all live with the results for a decade. After a decade, the issue can be put on the table again.

The Swiss practice a form of direct democracy. Between 1892 and 2004, Swiss citizens put more than 240 initiatives to public referendum. The populace has been conservative, approving only 14 of the initiatives put before them; in addition, they have sometimes opted for versions of initiatives rewritten by government personnel.[3]

The United States has a sort of direct democracy at the state level. More than half the states, and many localities, provide for citizen-sponsored ballot initiatives or ballot measures. Nothing like this exists at the federal level, however.

THE ONLY VOICE THAT MATTERS

Politicians pass laws without consulting their constituents. They spend our money without consulting us. They lead us into wars without our consent. That our political system is set up in this fashion derives from the Founding Fathers' belief that the citizens of this country needed safeguards when making their own decisions. In fact, citizens are capable of and should be making their own decisions on matters that affect them.

In the end, we have just one inalienable right: the right to decide our fate for ourselves. America belongs to its citizens. The Constitution is not an antique document but the will and wishes of the people. Our voice is the only voice that matters. If we don't like something, we can change it.

Politicians are public servants. They work for us; we do not work for them. If they are not doing their jobs to our satisfaction, it is time we do the work for ourselves. As my father used to say, repeating a familiar "go-get-'em" American adage, "If you want something done, do it yourself." So it is with legislation.

Many people will argue that national voting is unworkable because, outside of Switzerland, it has never been tested. But remember the definition of insanity: doing the same thing over and over again and expecting different results. We keep voting into office politicians who don't look after the public's will as the public would like. A highway bill gets stuffed with pork that shouldn't be there. If Louisiana needs an infusion of aid after Hurricane Katrina, money should be put aside for that purpose only, not earmarked via footnote for additional uses. Is "business as usual" in our political government better than a system untried?

Politicians are keenly aware that public opinion is sovereign in this country. But when it comes to action, public opinion doesn't count for much. On innumerable occasions, judges and politicians have failed to do the bidding of the voices they hear. The news media believe they are taking the temperature of the American public by conducting endless polls. But polling is not voting. What is true is that politicians and judges have disregarded our wishes on many occasions, deeming them unconstitutional. And while they hide behind the Constitution, the real question remains: What is more sacred, a 200-year-old document or the wishes of 298 million Americans?

The time for talking and arguing is over. Now is the time for action. Now you must vote on the issues yourself. You must demand that the outcome of your votes be made law for ten years. Protests and dialogue are always allowed. But once the votes are counted and tabulated, no court challenge, no judge, no politician, and no private citizen should overturn the wishes of the people of the United States.

You will not only participate in this process, you will be the process. For the first time in American history, you will be in charge of your own destiny. If you don't vote, your voice will not be heard. It's time to untie the legal and congressional knot that has a stranglehold on our nation. The decisions that affect our lives and our futures are too important to be left in the hands of politicians or the courts. Only we can speak for ourselves.

GET OUT YOUR PENS AND PENCILS

All this said, we have a lot of work to do, so let's get started. Get out a sharpened pencil. The following pages present the most significant and controversial issues concerning American citizens today. Each issue is described, and the arguments for and against are summarized. Record your own opinion under the heading "Choose One." I'm suggesting you make your choices in pencil first in case you change your mind. Once you've made your choices, record them in ink on the perforated ballot at the end of the book or on a photocopy of the voter ballot (see pages 63 and 64). Write your name and address on the ballot after you've finished voting and mail it to

> The President of the United States of America
> The White House
> 1600 Pennsylvania Avenue, NW
> Washington, DC 20500

By doing this you are demanding that *your* president make your wishes into law. Remember that we elected this individual and, like it or not, he has to listen to us and take action. He must then take steps to make sure our wishes become law.

Abortion

✻ ✻ ✻

ABORTION is the termination of a fetus within the first trimester of pregnancy (early abortion); abortions in the second or third trimester are called late-term abortions.

FOR
Abortion is a woman's right to choose. As long as abortion is legal, as it now is, what she does with her body is completely up to her.

AGAINST
The willful termination of human life at any stage of pregnancy goes against God's will and constitutes murder.

✓ CHOOSE ONE

> Should abortion continue to be sanctioned by the state?
>
> YES ❏   NO ❏

Affirmative Action

AFFIRMATIVE action generally means giving preferential treatment to minorities in admission to universities or employment in government and businesses. Affirmative action policies were originally developed to correct decades of discrimination and to give disadvantaged minorities a boost. The diversity of our current society compared with that of fifty years ago seems to indicate that such programs have been a success.

FOR

All people should be treated equally and fairly. Diversity is desirable and won't always occur if left to chance. Affirmative action draws people to areas of work they might never consider otherwise. Some stereotypes may never be broken without affirmative action. Affirmative action is needed to compensate minorities for centuries of slavery or oppression.

AGAINST

No segment of the population should be singled out for special treatment based on race or ethnicity. An individual should be appointed to a position based on his or her qualifications. Affirmative action leads to reverse discrimination. Affirmative action lowers the standards of accountability needed to push students or employees to perform better. To imply that they need affirmative action to succeed is condescending to minorities. When success is labeled as the result of affirmative action rather than hard work and ability, true minority achievement is demeaned.

✓ **CHOOSE ONE**

> Should affirmative action policies, which give preferential treatment based on minority status, be protected?
>
> YES ❏   NO ❏

Alcohol & Tobacco Prohibition

ALCOHOL and tobacco are drugs that have been enjoyed in our country for centuries. They are both currently legal, though the use of either can impair the judgment of the user, whose actions may have ramifications for others.

FOR

Prohibiting alcohol and tobacco use would save tens of thousands of lives each year in our country. Alcohol is to blame for more than 16,000 deaths on American roads annually, according to statistics compiled by the National Highway Traffic Safety Administration (NHTSA) and reported on the Mothers Against Drunk Driving Web site.[4] Of the 6,409 traffic fatalities involving young people between the ages of fifteen and twenty in 2003, 2,283 were alcohol related.[5] With teenagers having easy access to liquor, alcoholism begins early in our society.

Tobacco, nicknamed "the killer weed," is directly responsible for nearly half a million deaths a year in the United States.[6] Our taxes subsidize tobacco farmers, and these subsidies should end.

AGAINST

Prohibition in the 1920s did nothing to curb alcohol intake. In fact, it had the opposite effect. It sent America on one of the biggest drinking binges it has ever known. It also spawned organized crime, making those who trafficked in illegal alcohol incredibly wealthy. It is an adult's prerogative to decide whether to consume legal drugs. Millions of Americans enjoy tobacco and alcohol; legislating lifestyle and morality is a waste of time and a poor use of taxpayers' money.

✓ **CHOOSE ONE**

Should alcohol and tobacco be prohibited?

YES ❏   NO ❏

Amending the Constitution

THE Constitution of the United States of America guarantees us certain rights and liberties. Since it was written, it has been amended twenty-seven times, including the first ten amendments, called the Bill of Rights. At issue is whether any other amendments should be allowed.

FOR

The Constitution is not an antique document but a sacred expression of the wishes and will of the American people. The Founding Fathers dealt with problems very different from those we have today. Two centuries ago, we fought the tyranny of the British, who imposed unfair taxes upon the colonies. Today we fret over the scourge of higher taxes and the rising price of healthcare. At issue here is whether the thoughts and philosophies generated in eighteenth-century America are still relevant. Thomas Jefferson, the architect of the Constitution, was acutely aware of the need to reevaluate the underpinnings of the country. He suggested that the Constitution be revisited every twenty years.

AGAINST

The Constitution is a sacred document that in no way should be tampered with. It has protected us since the founding of the country and has enough flexibility built into it to continue working even if it is never changed. Changing interpretations of the material in the Constitution keep it alive and well.

✓ CHOOSE ONE

Should changes or further amendments to the Constitution of the United States of America be allowed by law?

YES ❏   NO ❏

Capital Punishment

WHEN a person commits a heinous crime such as first-degree murder or treason, the offense might warrant "special circumstances," which means that the state can take the life of that individual by execution.

FOR

Capital punishment deters potential murderers and should be mandated by the government. It protects innocent people by eliminating the most violent criminals, and it helps victims' families by providing retribution. Capital punishment shows criminals that there is a price to pay for serious wrongdoing.

AGAINST

Taking a person's life in retribution for a crime is just as barbaric and inhumane as the original crime and is itself murder. On its Web page entitled "Facts about Deterrence and the Death Penalty," the Death Penalty Information Center, a nonprofit organization that studies issues pertaining to capital punishment, cites myriad studies that attest to the fact that capital punishment does not deter crime.[7] Life is sacred; mistakes are made and innocent people are executed. Life imprisonment without the possibility of parole is a much more appropriate sentence than the death penalty even for the crime of murder.

✓ CHOOSE ONE

Should capital punishment be mandated by law?

YES ❏   NO ❏

Electoral College

THE Electoral College formally elects the president of the United States. American voters do not vote directly for the president but for members of the Electoral College. If a candidate wins a certain number of votes in a particular state, the candidate wins the electors and carries the state.

FOR

Whether or not the original purposes of the Electoral College might be considered antiquated, this method of tabulating votes in a presidential election works. This voting method has run smoothly for more than two hundred years; any other system would be cumbersome.

AGAINST

Voting is our most sacred right; every individual vote should count. The majority of the people who cast their ballots on November 7, 2000, cast them in favor of one man, who won the popular vote by just under 400,000 votes but who lost the election because he didn't carry the states' electoral votes. That election was not decided by the people of this country but by five justices of the Supreme Court who voted along party lines. If there was any doubt that the votes of the people of this nation do not count, the 2000 election demonstrated that they do not. The Electoral College has got to go.

✓ CHOOSE ONE

Should the Electoral College be retained?

YES ❑   NO ❑

Entitlements (Social Security & Welfare)

SOCIAL Security and welfare are considered entitlements. Social Security provides retirement income to American citizens over the age of sixty-five who have contributed to the program during their working years. Welfare is financial assistance provided to people whose income falls below a certain level.

FOR
We are entitled to Social Security and welfare income because our taxes fund these programs.

AGAINST
Entitlements breed laziness and complacency. Social Security is probably going to go bankrupt in another decade, and we could halve our tax burden by getting rid of public assistance altogether. We have become a welfare state to the degree that welfare subsidizes illegitimacy, encouraging young women to get pregnant in order to get welfare money.

✓ CHOOSE ONE

Should entitlements be maintained?

YES ❑   NO ❑

Foreign Aid

Foreign aid is the donation of money and supplies (medical, food, military) to countries outside the United States.

FOR

It is paramount that we give vast quantities of funds, food, arms, and medicine to countries in need. Foreign aid not only helps the country in question, it also helps in stabilizing the rest of the world politically. Without foreign aid, many countries would dissolve into a welter of chaos and civil war that could have an impact outside their borders, destabilizing entire regions. Israel is a good example. Without foreign aid, this vital Middle Eastern country would be in dire jeopardy.

AGAINST

Charity begins at home. Tens of thousands of people in this country are homeless and in want of food and shelter and basic provisions. Before the needs of others abroad are met, ours at home must first be taken care of. The billions of dollars that are sent overseas to assist people in other countries must be spent first on those who are in need in our own country.

✓ **CHOOSE ONE**

Should foreign aid continue?

YES ❏   NO ❏

Foster Care

THE system known as foster care allows the courts to remove children at risk from their families of birth and place them with other families appointed by the court.

FOR

Lacking orphanages or other institutions to care for abused or unwanted children, the foster care system is the best one we have outside of adoption. Children go into foster care only in extreme situations—parents die or are incarcerated and there are no living relatives to care for the children, or the children are abused by or suspected of being abused by their parents. Foster care is useful as a temporary measure for children with no other place to safely live.

AGAINST

The foster care system allows children to be bounced from one foster home to another, from one set of strangers to another. The system is untenable at best. Too many children in foster care are abused by their foster parents. Children at risk would be better off if they could go to orphanages with stable caretaking staffs as in the past.

✓ **CHOOSE ONE**

Should the foster care system be maintained?

YES ❏   NO ❏

Free Speech

THE First Amendment to the Constitution guarantees us the right of free speech and free expression. It does not, however, allow reckless behavior. We are not free to shout "fire" in a crowded theater when there is no threat or to shout "bomb" on a commercial airliner.

FOR

Free speech is an essential ingredient of American life. It is part of our history. The Constitution automatically guarantees us our freedom of expression.

AGAINST

Much of the moral decay that has occurred in our country can be directly blamed on violent films and videos and pornography that are protected under the guise of free speech and free expression. As a first measure in protecting our children, freedom of speech and expression should be curtailed.

✓ CHOOSE ONE

Should freedom of speech always be protected?

YES ❏   NO ❏

Gambling

ALTHOUGH legal in some states, most gambling in the United States is against state or federal law.

FOR

Gambling is a pastime enjoyed by millions of adults in our country. It is a pleasurable form of recreation and should be legal nationwide so people can play private card games and place sports bets without having to anxiously look over their shoulders. Also, the taxes generated from legal gambling provides many states with much-needed additional revenue.

AGAINST

Gambling is a form of addiction like drug use. People need to be protected from their own destructive behaviors. Gambling must be banned. Only through complete prohibition can people be saved from this scourge.

✓ CHOOSE ONE

> Should gambling be legalized nationwide?
>
> YES ❏   NO ❏

Gun Banning

★ ★ ★

GUN banning is the most extreme form of gun control. While gun control restricts the purchase of certain types of firearms to certain individuals, banning prohibits the possession of all firearms except by military and law enforcement personnel.

FOR

The statistics speak for themselves: More than 30,000 Americans were injured by firearms in 2002, according to the National Vital Statistics Report.[8] Guns are involved in thousands of senseless murders in this country every year. With easy access to firearms, children are killing children in schools throughout the nation. At home, children are accidentally killed by guns careless parents fail to lock up. According to the Centers for Disease Control and Prevention, firearms injuries remain a leading cause of death in the United States, particularly among youth.[9]

AGAINST

The Second Amendment gives all American citizens the right to bear arms. Shooting is a national pastime, whether for hunting or target shooting. Guns are also indispensable for self-defense. Countless lives are saved each year by gun owners who use their weapons to protect themselves. In the time it can take police to respond to a 911 emergency call, home invasion intruders, rapists, and murderers will have already committed their crimes. The best defensive tool against these lethal threats is a gun.

✓ CHOOSE ONE

Should guns be banned?

YES ❑   NO ❑

Illegal Immigration

A person who enters the United States without our government's knowledge or permission or stays beyond the termination date of a visa is engaging in illegal immigration. The most common form of illegal immigration is crossing over the U.S. border from either Canada or Mexico.

FOR

Most American citizens do not want the low-paying, labor-intensive jobs available to workers who seek illegal refuge in this country in order to work, but these jobs are crucial to our economy. Exceptions must be made to allow illegal immigrants to work in this country. Documents granting work rights and drivers' licenses should not be denied to immigrants just because of their illegal status.

AGAINST

Breaking any American law must not be tolerated. American citizens who unlawfully enter a foreign country are subject to deportation. Foreigners who enter the United States illegally should likewise be deported.

✓ CHOOSE ONE

Should illegal immigration be tolerated?

YES ❏   NO ❏

Mandatory National Service

MANDATORY national service would direct all young men and women between the ages of eighteen and twenty-six to serve two years in a branch of the armed forces.

FOR

Mandatory national service is an effective way to secure the numbers we need in the armed forces to protect our country.

AGAINST

To require people to do national service harks back to the draft and the Vietnam era. A volunteer army is better suited for combat than a drafted one.

✓ CHOOSE ONE

Should national service be mandatory?

YES ❑   NO ❑

Medicaid

MEDICAID is a program sponsored by the federal government and administered by the states that is intended to provide healthcare and health-related services to low-income individuals who can't afford to pay for their own healthcare.

FOR

The Medicaid system is a blessing. It gives the poor in this country free access to medical care.

AGAINST

Our tax dollars are being eaten up by a medical system that does not work, and adding free care for the poor on top of that is an economic disaster.

✔ CHOOSE ONE

Should Medicaid be preserved?

YES ❑   NO ❑

Military Spending

MILITARY spending is the amount of money we spend not only on our own army and arsenals but also on equipment and services we donate to other countries. The cost of wars and conflicts we are engaged in is tallied into our military spending.

FOR

Massive military spending, including the money we give to foreign allies, has made our nation safer. It has helped to prevent another 9/11-type terrorist attack.

AGAINST

We can achieve our political aims in better ways than through military action of our own or funding that of foreign friends. We could, for instance, strengthen security and tighten the nets that prevent terrorists from entering our country. Money would be better spent securing our borders. Our foreign policy could make more use of diplomacy and the United Nations so that our military would rarely be deployed in combat.

✓ CHOOSE ONE

Should we continue to fund military spending at or above the levels we have funded it for the past fifty years?

YES ❏   NO ❏

Narcotics Decriminalization

NARCOTICS such as cocaine, marijuana, and heroin are illegal in this country for the very reason that they are considered to be dangerous. They have the potential to destroy lives and cause death.

FOR

The decriminalization of illegal drugs would benefit society. Drug taking is a personal choice, no different from cigarette smoking or alcohol consumption. Prohibition is a losing battle; we need look no further than the failure of alcohol prohibition during the 1920s in our country to see how a law meant to do good did harm.

A much better avenue than criminalization is toleration. Consider the Dutch model, which has yielded positive results in the war against drugs. Holland tolerates all the substances that we don't, yet it does not have the level of crime we have. In the United States, state and federal governments spend more than $40 billion a year on the war against drugs. That money would be better spent on education and drug treatment.

AGAINST

Illegal narcotics are the cause of thousands of deaths each year in this country. If made legal, their use would increase and the number of overdoses would rise. Also, the drugs would find their way into the hands of children much more readily. It is very clear that people need to be protected from themselves.

✓ CHOOSE ONE

Should narcotics be decriminalized?

YES ❏   NO ❏

National Debt

THE national debt, which might better be termed the "federal debt," is the total amount of money the federal government has borrowed from institutions and individuals—not just in one year, but the total for all the years it has been in existence—and has not yet repaid.

FOR

While it would be nice to reduce or eliminate the national debt, our economy has always survived it. If the federal government requires additional capital in distressed periods, it should be allowed access to such funds.

AGAINST

The national debt should be eliminated. Just as we must be responsible for balancing our own checkbooks, so should the federal government be accountable in restraining its zealous overspending.

✓ CHOOSE ONE

Should the national debt be allowed to continue?

YES ❏   NO ❏

National Identity Card

A national identity card would identify U.S. citizens as Americans. While similar to a passport that allows citizens to travel abroad, a national identity card cannot be used outside the country. The card is designed simply for the purpose of verifying identity.

FOR

Billions of taxpayers' dollars are being spent on medical care and education for illegal immigrants. A national identity card would help to distinguish a citizen from an illegal alien at the time of medical treatment, employment, or school enrollment. Apart from our passports, we have no documentation to distinguish us as Americans. Most Americans do not have U.S. passports, and those who do are rarely asked to produce them inside the country for the purpose of identification. Passports are intended only for travel outside the United States.

AGAINST

A national identity card requirement would violate our civil rights and our right to privacy. It would also be a complete waste of time because, like a lot of other official documents, a national identity card could easily be forged.

✓ CHOOSE ONE

Should a national identity card be implemented?

YES ❏   NO ❏

National Language

A national language is a single language used for all of a country's official communication.

FOR

We live in America, and in this country we speak English. Using one language, and one language only, would ease the congestion created by two languages being spoken in many businesses and branches of government. Millions of dollars could be saved annually in this country if a national language were instituted. Voting ballots, driving tests and manuals, and countless other state and federal pamphlets are currently printed in several languages, all at great taxpayer expense. This is a waste. If people become naturalized citizens of the United States of America, they need to learn to speak, read, and write English so as not to burden the system with multiple languages.

AGAINST

Although a single national language would be a good idea, it is already too late to turn the clock back. Most businesses and government agencies are already equipped to accommodate both Spanish- and English-speaking customers.

✔ CHOOSE ONE

Should a single national language be instituted?

YES ❏   NO ❏

Pornography

PORNOGRAPHY is any sexually explicit writing and/or picture intended to arouse sexual desire.

FOR

Pornography is a form of expression that is protected under the First Amendment. It is a form of expression that is enjoyed by millions of adults in this country. Google reports that every day, 68 million searches include some variation of the word "porn."[10] Clearly people want it. Parents must take responsibility to monitor their children's viewing habits to ensure that they are not exposed to pornography.

AGAINST

Pornography has no place in our lives. It has no place in the economy of the country. It has the potential to corrupt our children or, worse, cause them genuine harm. The statistics are staggering: more than 4.2 million Web sites are devoted to pornographic content.[11] Pornography is an ever-growing threat and needs to be stamped out.

✓ CHOOSE ONE

Should pornography be legal?

YES ❏   NO ❏

Prostitution

PROSTITUTION is the performance of sexual acts for money.

FOR

Prostitution is the "world's oldest profession" for a reason, and it is unlikely that any individual or government will ever successfully stamp it out. One reason is that legislating a consensual transaction between adults is virtually impossible.

Prior to the early twentieth century, prostitution was tolerated nationwide. Today's rise in crime rate is due not only to drug prohibition but also to the banning of prostitution. Holland provides a good example. The Dutch government turned prostitution into a business and a tourist attraction by legalizing it for anyone eighteen or older who acts freely, not under coercion.[12] In countries like Holland that tolerate prostitution, the law recognizes the impossibility of legislating sex.[13] Like pornography, prostitution is a pastime enjoyed by tens of thousands of Americans, despite the fact that it is illegal (except in some Nevada counties). (The exact number of patrons is unknowable, but consider that the Manhattan Yellow Pages had fifty-two pages of listings of escort services in 1998.[14])

AGAINST

Like pornography, prostitution has no place in our society. And like pornography, it has the potential to corrupt our children. Prostitution is an eyesore that pollutes entire neighborhoods.

✓ CHOOSE ONE

Should prostitution be legal?

YES ❏   NO ❏

Public School Financing

EVERY child in this nation is assured an education through secondary school. Paid for by taxpayers, this guarantee is one of the benefits of life in the United States.

FOR

Not enough money is spent on education. The physical plants of our public schools are in disrepair; some are even falling down. In many instances, schools cannot afford to purchase textbooks for students or classroom use. A major infusion of funds is necessary to make our schools first-rate again so that our children can read, write, and manipulate numbers comfortably.

AGAINST

Our public educational system receives adequate funding to maintain necessary educational standards. If problems exist, they are due to fiscal mismanagement on the part of local school districts.

✓ CHOOSE ONE

Should more money be spent on the public school system?

YES ❏   NO ❏

Separation of Church & State

THE principle behind the separation of church and state, a phrase first used by Thomas Jefferson, was to preserve and protect religious liberty. The Constitution placed limits on the government's power to legislate about matters of religion, which the First Amendment codified by explicitly stating that Congress must not make any laws to establish a state religion or prohibit the free exercise of religion.

FOR

God has no place in courtrooms, public schools, public buildings, or public monuments. Government and religion should be separate and not allowed to interfere in each other's affairs. A separation between the two is necessary to protect religious tolerance.

AGAINST

No real division exists between church and state, which is as it should be. Since the mid-1950s, God has been defined as the highest ruling authority in the nation. In court, we swear by Almighty God to tell the truth. God is in our Pledge of Allegiance, and the motto "In God We Trust" is on all U.S. currency.

✓ CHOOSE ONE

Should a division be upheld between church and state?

YES ❏   NO ❏

Taxation

TAXES are involuntary fees paid by individuals or businesses to a government. Sales taxes are added to the price of most goods we buy and services we use. Income taxes are levied each year to pay for items such as military spending, public school education, Social Security, and welfare.

FOR

Our current system of taxation works fine, although the rich do not pay their fair share and it would be better if personal and corporate income taxes for the highest wage earners were set at a mandatory 50 percent.

AGAINST

The current system of personal income taxation does not work. The system is too complicated, and the Internal Revenue Service is too intrusive in its ways of collecting income taxes. Basically, in order to pay their tax debt each year, most Americans have to work forty-three days for the IRS. Many creative ways have been suggested to generate revenue without encroaching on our personal income or our privacy. The IRS should probably be abolished and replaced by a national lottery or a national sales tax. If the people felt that the IRS must play a part in income and corporate taxation, a simple flat tax of 5 percent without any deductions could be applied to everyone. Perhaps even a combination of all these ways of collecting money might be implemented.

✔ CHOOSE ONE

Should the current system of taxation be maintained?

YES ❏   NO ❏

Terrorism & Antiterrorist Measures

✯ ✯ ✯

TERRORISM is the unlawful use—or threatened use—of force or violence against individuals or property to coerce or intimidate governments or societies, often to achieve political, religious, or ideological objectives.

FOR

Guaranteeing our national security is paramount, and bombing and invading countries that promote terrorism is justified in order to ensure our security. Any measure is warranted in order to guarantee our national security, including the detention of individuals, even American citizens, without due process if they act suspiciously.

AGAINST

The American social and political system depends on the protection afforded its citizens as put forth in the Constitution and the Bill of Rights. Clamping down on free speech, freedom of expression, and due process compromises the American way of life. In our current political climate, it is popular to blame terrorists and terrorism for the world's ills, but it is important that we take responsibility for the role we play and defend ourselves against terrorism without harming our own political system.

✓ CHOOSE ONE

Should antiterrorist measures be enacted and kept in place for the foreseeable future?

YES ❑   NO ❑

Universal Healthcare

A universal healthcare system ensures that all citizens receive complete healthcare and all necessary medications without any direct costs to them.

FOR

Universal healthcare is a system that is long overdue in our country to ease the financial strain of medical expenses shouldered by millions of Americans. While it is true that taxes would have to be raised, the money that would fund the program could come from a variety of sources, not just personal income taxes. The British National Health Service, for instance, is funded jointly by a health insurance tax and by the national treasury.[15] In our country, 50 percent of all consumer bankruptcies are caused by health-related issues.[16] This is just one way that, as a society, we pay a high cost for not providing healthcare for all citizens.

AGAINST

Such a plan would burden our economy. Taxes would soar in order to fund this plan. It is possible that without the economic incentive that now motivates many drug makers, medical research and innovation would dry up altogether if universal healthcare were instituted.[17]

✓ **CHOOSE ONE**

Should a universal healthcare system for every American be implemented?

YES ❏   NO ❏

Voluntary Euthanasia

VOLUNTARY euthanasia would make it legal for a competent adult suffering unbearably from an incurable illness, whose quality of life has become severely compromised, to receive medical help to die at his or her own considered and persistent request.

FOR

Issues of mortality are entirely up to each person to determine. If the quality of life is diminished by terminal illness, the choice to decide his or her own end belongs to the individual.

AGAINST

Legalizing voluntary euthanasia will encourage unscrupulous doctors who can abuse their power by "euthanizing" people inappropriately. From a legal perspective, voluntary euthanasia is the willful taking of a human life no matter what the patient's condition. It is tantamount to murder. From a religious perspective, when life should end is not up to the individual but to God.

✓ CHOOSE ONE

Should voluntary euthanasia be legal?

YES ❑   NO ❑

Take Action!

Congratulations. You have just reviewed and voted on the most important issues facing our country. Tear out the perforated ballot at the end of the book or photocopy the following voter ballot and mark your choices in ink and send it to

The President of the United States of America
The White House
1600 Pennsylvania Avenue, NW
Washington, DC 20500

You can also vote online at **http://www.howwouldyouvote.us**. Remember, these are your wishes. We need to remind the president that he must listen to the people of this country.

Abortion
Should abortion continue to be sanctioned by the state?

YES ○   NO ○

Affirmative Action
Should affirmative action policies, which give preferential treatment based on minority status, be protected?

YES ○   NO ○

Alcohol & Tobacco Prohibition
Should alcohol and tobacco be prohibited?

YES ○   NO ○

Amending the Constitution
Should changes or further amendments to the Constitution of the United States of America be allowed by law?

YES ○   NO ○

Capital Punishment
Should capital punishment be mandated by law?

YES ○   NO ○

Electoral College
Should the Electoral College be retained?

YES ○   NO ○

Entitlements (Social Security & Welfare)
Should entitlements be maintained?

YES ○   NO ○

Foreign Aid
Should foreign aid continue?

YES ○   NO ○

Foster Care
Should the foster care system be maintained?

YES ○   NO ○

Free Speech
Should freedom of speech always be protected?

YES ○   NO ○

Gambling
Should gambling be legalized nationwide?

YES ○   NO ○

Gun Banning
Should guns be banned?

YES ○   NO ○

Illegal Immigration
Should illegal immigration be tolerated?

YES ○   NO ○

Mandatory National Service
Should national service be mandatory?

YES ○   NO ○

Medicaid
Should Medicaid be preserved?

YES ○   NO ○

Military Spending
Should we continue to fund military spending at or above the levels we have funded it for the past fifty years?

YES ○   NO ○

Narcotics Decriminalization
Should narcotics be decriminalized?

YES ○   NO ○

National Debt
Should the national debt be allowed to continue?

YES ○   NO ○

National Identity Card
Should a national identity card be implemented?

YES ○   NO ○

National Language
Should a single national language be instituted?

YES ○   NO ○

Pornography
Should pornography be legal?

YES ○   NO ○

Prostitution
Should prostitution be legal?

YES ○   NO ○

Public School Financing
Should more money be spent on the public school system?

YES ○   NO ○

Separation of Church & State
Should a division be upheld between church and state?

YES ○   NO ○

Taxation
Should the current system of taxation be maintained?

YES ○   NO ○

Terrorism & Anti-terrorist Measures
Should antiterrorist measures be enacted and kept in place for the foreseeable future?

YES ○   NO ○

Universal Healthcare
Should a universal healthcare system for every American be implemented?

YES ○   NO ○

Voluntary Euthanasia
Should voluntary euthanasia be legal?

YES ○   NO ○

How Would You Vote If You Were Allowed To? by W. R. Wilkerson III © 2006

PLACE
FIRST-CLASS
STAMP
HERE

The President of the United States
The White House
1600 Pennsylvania Avenue NW
Washington, DC 20500

Name: _____

Address: _____
　　　　　_____

Dear Mr. President,

Please review my ballot and then deliver it to the General Accounting Office to be tabulated with the others like it. Whatever the outcome of the vote, we demand that our wishes be enacted into law.

Appendices

RAZOR THIN VICTORIES AND OTHER CLOSE ELECTION CALLS

Separating fact from fiction in the one-vote arena is hard: the idea that one vote can change history is such an appealing notion, it's offered as a lure to get people out to the polls. Mixed in with real razor thin victories are many claims that sound good but simply aren't true: One claim, widely reported, is that one vote made English the official language of America instead of German in 1776. Another, equally widely reported, is that in 1923, one vote gave Adolf Hitler leadership of the Nazi Party. Unfortunately, fun as these are to contemplate, snopes.com calls them urban legends pure and simple: neither of them checks out as actually having happened.

But many close election calls do check out—incidents that show how individual votes really do matter. Consider the following examples.

In 2000, President George Bush won the presidential election by only 537 votes (some sources say 527). This election was one of the few times in United States history that a candidate won the presidency while losing the nationwide popular vote. The contest hinged on Florida, where that state's 25 electoral votes were decided by an official vote count of 537 (some say 527) in favor of Bush out of a Florida total of about 6 million votes. In the end, court cases decided the election, but a few thousand votes one way or another in Florida would have brought a concession speech by one of the contenders and avoided a court-decided victory.[18]

A one-vote victory that snopes.com reports is fact, not fiction, was won by Marcus "Landslide" Morton in 1839 when he was elected governor of Massachusetts by one vote. He received 51,034 of the 102,066 votes cast. Had the vote been tied at 51,033, the election would have been decided in the legislature, which would probably have chosen his opponent. Amazingly, in 1842, Landslide did it again, winning the same office by one vote in the legislature.

In 1845, one vote brought Texas into the Union. When all attempts to arrive at a formal annexation treaty had failed, the U.S. Congress passed a joint resolution for annexing Texas to the United States. In the Senate, the vote for annexation was tied at twenty-six until Henry S. Johnson of Louisiana switched sides and voted in favor of the resolution. Thus, Texas statehood via annexation is said to be the result of a single vote, supported by the evidence in the Texas State Library and Archives Commission.[19]

Another one-vote fact endorsed by snopes.com is that one vote saved President Andrew Johnson from being removed from office in 1868. The Senate failed by just one vote to convict Johnson of attempting to undermine Congress, the site reports. As a result of this and another motion a short time later, which again failed by just one vote, he was not removed from office.[20]

OTHER CLOSE CALLS

In November 2005, Michael Sessions, an eighteen-year-old high school senior, won the mayoral race in the small town of Hillsdale, Michigan (population 9,000), by beating the fifty-one-year-old incumbent 732 to 668.[21] Not one vote, but very close. Sessions ran as a write-in candidate because initially he was too young to be placed on the ballot. He used $700 from a summer job to fund his door-to-door campaign.

In Alaska in 1978, Jay Hammond was nominated for governor when he got just ninety-eight votes more than his opponent, Walter Hickel, in the primary. "That's less than one-quarter vote per precinct!" reports the Alaska lieutenant governor's office.[22]

Alaska keeps a keen eye on its close elections and reports that one vote elected Tim Kelly to his state senate seat in 1978. In 1982, in the primaries, David McCracken won the nomination for state senate by two votes. In 1984, Mary Ratcliff won the nomination for state representative by one vote. In 1986, Rick Uehling was elected to the state senate by less than one vote per precinct, only 17 votes out of 14,389. In 1992, Al Vezey won the nomination for state representative by five votes, again less than one vote per precinct. Two years later, Tony Knowles was elected governor and Fran Ulmer lieutenant governor by 1.1 votes per precinct. And in 1996, Ann Spohnholz won the nomination for state representative by one vote.[23]

Iowa also keeps close tabs on its elections. In 1986, the Iowa House of Representatives passed a measure that changed the legal drinking age in the state from nineteen to twenty-one by one vote. In 1989, the Iowa Senate and House passed a measure by one vote in each chamber that allowed riverboat gambling in the state. In 1988, one vote won Bob Hellyer the Democratic nomination for Iowa House District 67. Less than one vote per precinct won Keith Kreiman the Democratic nomination for Iowa House District 92. Two votes per precinct won Christopher Rants the Republican nomination for House District 2 the same year. In 1996, by getting less than one vote each in half of the precincts in Iowa Senate District 30, Neal Schuerer won the Republican primary. He went on to win the seat in the general election. Less than two votes per precinct got Governor Thomas Vilsack the Democratic nomination for governor. Karen Balderston won the Republican primary for Iowa House District 36 with less than one vote per precinct.[24]

Want more evidence that your vote is important? The National Court Reporters Association looked into the "one vote matters" claims and came up with these examples.[25]

In 1829, Nicholas Coleman of Kentucky was elected to the U.S. House of Representatives by one vote, 2,520 to 2,519. In Indiana in 1847, George G. Dunn, a Whig, was elected to the House of Representatives by one vote, 7,455 to 7,454. That same year, another Whig, Thomas S. Flournoy of Virginia, also won a seat in the House by one vote. One vote won James C. Allen of Illinois his seat in the House in 1854 and did the same for Robert M. Mayo of Virginia in 1882.

More recently, Sydney Nixon took his seat as a Vermont state representative in 1977, having apparently won the election, 570 to 569. However, a recount determined that he had in fact lost to Robert Emond, 572 to 571, and Nixon resigned.

In Michigan in 1989, the Lansing School District had to reduce its budget by $2.5 million when the final recount for a millage proposition resulted in a tie vote, 5,147 to 5,147. In the original count, the proposition lost by only ten votes.

In 1994, a Ping Pong ball settled the race between Randall Luthi and Larry Call for a seat in the Wyoming House of Representatives. The original count was tied at 1,941 votes each. When a recount also resulted in a tie, the State Canvassing Board held a drawing to decide the winner. A

Ping Pong ball with Luthi's name on it was drawn from a cowboy hat belonging to the governor, Mike Sullivan, and Luthi won the seat.

In South Dakota in 1997, the race for the second seat in Legislative District 12 was another close one. On election night, John McIntyre had 4,195 votes to Hal Wick's 4,191. However, a recount showed Wick was the winner, 4,192 votes to 4,191. When the state supreme court ruled that an overvote made one ballot cast for Wick invalid, the race was a tie. The state legislature finally voted 46–20 to give the election to Wick.

The closest House election in 1998 was won by Donald Sherwood from Pennsylvania, who was elected by 515 votes, less than one vote per precinct. Leslie Byrne became a Virginia state senator by 37 votes, less than one vote per precinct, in 1999.[26]

On July 25, 2003, the House passed by only one vote a Republican plan that would dismantle Head Start, the nation's premiere early childhood education program for low-income children.[27]

In Virginia, just twenty-four voters could have changed the results of five local elections in November 2005, writes Calvin R. Trice in the *Richmond Times-Dispatch*. "All those adults with potentially decisive votes could fit comfortably in a school classroom, where one person could give them a civics lesson: In the Jackson River District seat for the Alleghany Board of Supervisors, the difference was a single vote. That race could have been knotted by any registered voter who drove past his precinct by chance, realized it was Election Day, but didn't stop because he figured the lines were too long." Although thousands of votes were cast across the state, races in Alleghany, Charlotte, Clarke, Craig, and Shenandoah counties were won by mere handfuls of votes. Those elections were decided "not by those who didn't show up to vote, but those who did."[28]

In New Hampshire in 1974, a close race for a U.S. Senate seat, between Democrat John Durkin and Republican Louis Wyman, was decided by a handful of votes. A recount reported a mere ten votes in favor of Durkin, reversing an earlier narrow result in favor of Wyman. A second recount went in favor of Wyman by two votes. Finally, after a year of controversy and wrangling in court, John Durkin won the special election to settle the matter.[29]

In Milltown, New Jersey, Randy Farkas, a Republican, was declared the winner in a race for borough council seat in the November 2005 election by one vote over his Democratic opponent, Joseph Cruz. "It is a great civics lesson," Farkas told a reporter right after election night when the tally stood at 1,363 to 1,362. "It's just one of those other things that we take for granted; one vote really does matter."[30] Eight days later, after 20 absentee ballots were counted, the vote shifted toward Cruz, making him the official winner, 1,369 to 1,368. Cruz called his victory "bittersweet." "Who wants to win an election like that?" he told a reporter from the local paper. "Election season is tough enough. This made it even tougher."[31]

The Nineteenth Amendment, which gave women the right to vote, was passed in Congress in 1919. Over the next fourteen months, it was ratified by thirty-six states. The final state, Tennessee, passed the measure by only one vote, cast by Harry Burn, a twenty-five-year-old legislator. Burn originally opposed the amendment, but a telegram from his mother changed his mind. Her message read, "Hurrah, and vote for suffrage!" This gleeful encouragement has been widely repeated, including on the National Women's History Project's Web site celebrating the eighty-fifth anniversary of the passage of the amendment.[32]

The Constitution of the United States

We the people of the United States, in order to form a more perfect Union, establish justice, insure domestic tranquility, provide for the common defense, promote the general welfare, and secure the blessings of liberty to ourselves and our posterity, do ordain and establish this Constitution for the United States of America.

ARTICLE I
Section 1.
All legislative powers herein granted shall be vested in a Congress of the United States, which shall consist of a Senate and House of Representatives.

Section 2.
The House of Representatives shall be composed of members chosen every second year by the people of the several States, and the electors in each State shall have the qualifications requisite for electors of the most numerous branch of the State Legislature.

No person shall be a Representative who shall not have attained to the age of twenty five years, and been seven years a citizen of the United States, and who shall not, when elected, be an inhabitant of that State in which he shall be chosen.

Representatives and direct taxes shall be apportioned among the several States which may be included within this Union, according to their respective numbers, which shall be determined by adding to the whole number of free persons, including those bound to service for a term of years, and excluding Indians not taxed, three fifths of all other Persons. The actual enumeration shall be made within three years after the first meeting of the Congress of the United States, and within every subsequent term of ten years, in such manner as they shall by law direct. The number of Representatives shall not exceed one for every thirty thousand, but each State shall have at least one Representative; and until such enumeration shall be made, the State of New Hampshire shall be entitled to choose three, Massachusetts eight, Rhode Island and Providence Plantations one, Connecticut five, New York six, New Jersey four, Pennsylvania eight, Delaware one, Maryland six, Virginia ten, North Carolina five, South Carolina five, and Georgia three.

When vacancies happen in the representation from any State, the Executive Authority thereof shall issue writs of election to fill such vacancies.

The House of Representatives shall choose their Speaker and other officers; and shall have the sole power of impeachment.

Section 3.
The Senate of the United States shall be composed of two Senators from each State, chosen by the Legislature thereof, for six years; and each Senator shall have one vote.

Immediately after they shall be assembled in consequence of the first election, they shall be divided as equally as may be into three classes. The seats of the Senators of the first class shall be vacated at the expiration of the second year, of the second class at the expiration of the fourth year, and the third class at the expiration of the sixth year, so that one third may be chosen every second year; and if vacancies happen by resignation, or otherwise, during the recess of the Legislature of any state, the executive thereof may make temporary appointments until the next meeting of the Legislature, which shall then fill such vacancies.

No person shall be a Senator who shall not have attained to the age of thirty years, and been nine years a citizen of the United States, and who shall not, when elected, be an inhabitant of that state for which he shall be chosen.

The Vice President of the United States shall be President of the Senate, but shall have no vote, unless they be equally divided.

The Senate shall choose their other officers, and also a President pro tempore, in the absence of the Vice President, or when he shall exercise the office of President of the United States.

The Senate shall have the sole power to try all impeachments. When sitting for that purpose, they shall be on oath or affirmation. When the President of the United States is tried, the Chief Justice shall preside: And no person shall be convicted without the concurrence of two thirds of the members present.

Judgment in cases of impeachment shall not extend further than to removal from office, and disqualification to hold and enjoy any office of honor, trust or profit under the United States: but the party convicted shall nevertheless be liable and subject to indictment, trial, judgment and punishment, according to law.

Section 4.
The times, places and manner of holding elections for Senators and Representatives, shall be prescribed in each State by the Legislature thereof; but the Congress may at any time by law make or alter such regulations, except as to the places of choosing Senators.

The Congress shall assemble at least once in every year, and such meeting shall be on the first Monday in December, unless they shall by law appoint a different day.

Section 5.
Each House shall be the judge of the elections, returns and qualifications of its own members, and a majority of each shall constitute a quorum to do business; but a smaller number may adjourn from day to day, and may be authorized to compel the attendance of absent members, in such manner, and under such penalties as each House may provide.

Each House may determine the rules of its proceedings, punish its members for disorderly behavior, and, with the concurrence of two thirds, expel a member.

Each House shall keep a journal of its proceedings, and from time to time publish the same, excepting such parts as may in their judgment require secrecy; and the yeas and nays of the members of either House on any question shall, at the desire of one fifth of those present, be entered on the journal.

Neither House, during the session of Congress, shall, without the consent of the other, adjourn for more than three days, nor to any other place than that in which the two Houses shall be sitting.

Section 6.
The Senators and Representatives shall receive a compensation for their services, to be ascertained by law, and paid out of the Treasury of the United States. They shall in all cases, except treason, felony and breach of the peace, be privileged from arrest during their attendance at the session of their respective Houses, and in going to and returning from the same; and for any speech or debate in either House, they shall not be questioned in any other place.

No Senator or Representative shall, during the time for which he was elected, be appointed to any civil office under the authority of the United States, which shall have been created, or the emoluments whereof shall have been increased during such time; and no person holding any office under the United States, shall be a member of either House during his continuance in office.

Section 7.
All bills for raising revenue shall originate in the House of Representatives; but the Senate may propose or concur with amendments as on other Bills.

Every bill which shall have passed the House of Representatives and the Senate, shall, before it become a law, be presented to the president of the United States; if he approve he shall sign it, but if not he shall return it, with his objections to that house in which it shall have originated, who shall enter the objections at large on their journal, and proceed to reconsider it. If after such reconsideration two thirds of that house shall agree to pass the bill, it shall be sent, together with the objections, to the other house, by which it shall likewise be reconsidered, and if approved by two thirds of that house, it shall become a law. But in all such cases the votes of both houses shall be determined by yeas and nays, and the names of the persons voting for and against the bill shall be entered on the journal of each house respectively. If any bill shall not be returned by the President within ten days (Sundays excepted) after it shall have been presented to him, the same shall be a law, in like manner as if he had signed it, unless the Congress by their adjournment prevent its return, in which case it shall not be a law.

Every order, resolution, or vote to which the concurrence of the Senate and House of Representatives may be necessary (except on a question of adjournment) shall be presented to the president of the United States; and before the same shall take effect, shall be approved by him, or being disapproved by him, shall be repassed by two thirds of the Senate and House of Representatives, according to the rules and limitations prescribed in the case of a bill.

Section 8.
The Congress shall have power to lay and collect taxes, duties, imposts and excises, to pay the debts and provide for the common defence and general welfare of the United States; but all duties, imposts and excises shall be uniform throughout the United States;

To borrow money on the credit of the United States;

To regulate commerce with foreign nations, and among the several states, and with the Indian tribes;

To establish an uniform rule of naturalization, and uniform laws on the subject of bankruptcies throughout the United States;

To coin money, regulate the value thereof, and of foreign coin, and fix the standard of weights and measures;

To provide for the punishment of counterfeiting the securities and current coin of the United States;

To establish post offices and post roads;

To promote the progress of science and useful arts, by securing for limited times to authors and inventors the exclusive right to their respective writings and discoveries;

To constitute tribunals inferior to the supreme court;

To define and punish piracies and felonies committed on the high seas, and offences against the law of nations;

To declare war, grant letters of marque and reprisal, and make rules concerning captures on land and water;

To raise and support armies, but no appropriation of money to that use shall be for a longer term than two years;

To provide and maintain a navy;

To make rules for the government and regulation of the land and naval forces;

To provide for calling forth the militia to execute the laws of the union, suppress insurrections and repel invasions;

To provide for organizing, arming, and disciplining, the militia, and for governing such part of them as may be employed in the service of the United States, reserving to the states respectively, the appointment of the officers, and the authority of training the militia according to the discipline prescribed by Congress;

To exercise exclusive legislation in all cases whatsoever, over such district (not exceeding ten miles square) as may, by cession of particular states, and the acceptance of Congress, become the seat of the government of the United States, and to exercise like authority over all places purchased by the consent of the Legislature of the state in which the same shall be, for the erection of forts, magazines, arsenals, dockyards, and other needful buildings;—And

To make all laws which shall be necessary and proper for carrying into execution the foregoing powers, and all other powers vested by this constitution in the government of the United States, or in any department or officer thereof.

Section 9.
The migration or importation of such persons as any of the states now existing shall think proper to admit, shall not be prohibited by the Congress prior to the year one thousand eight hundred and eight, but a tax or duty may be imposed on such importation, not exceeding ten dollars for each person.

The privilege of the writ of habeas corpus shall not be suspended, unless when in cases of rebellion or invasion the public safety may require it.

No bill of attainder or ex post facto Law shall be passed.

No capitation, or other direct, tax shall be laid, unless in proportion to the census or enumeration herein before directed to be taken.

No tax or duty shall be laid on articles exported from any state.

No preference shall be given by any regulation of commerce or revenue to the ports of one state over those of another: nor shall vessels bound to, or from, one state, be obliged to enter, clear, or pay duties in another.

No money shall be drawn from the treasury, but in consequence of appropriations made by law; and a regular statement and account of receipts and expenditures of all public money shall be published from time to time.

No title of nobility shall be granted by the United States: And no person holding any office of profit or trust under them, shall, without the consent of the Congress, accept of any present, emolument, office, or title, of any kind whatever, from any king, prince, or foreign state.

Section 10.

No state shall enter into any treaty, alliance, or confederation; grant letters of marque and reprisal; coin money; emit bills of credit; make anything but gold and silver coin a tender in payment of debts; pass any bill of attainder, ex post facto law, or law impairing the obligation of contracts, or grant any title of nobility.

No state shall, without the consent of the Congress, lay any imposts or duties on imports or exports, except what may be absolutely necessary for executing it's inspection laws: and the net produce of all duties and imposts, laid by any state on imports or exports, shall be for the use of the treasury of the United States; and all such laws shall be subject to the revision and control of the Congress.

No state shall, without the consent of Congress, lay any duty of tonnage, keep troops, or ships of war in time of peace, enter into any agreement or compact with another state, or with a foreign power, or engage in war, unless actually invaded, or in such imminent danger as will not admit of delay.

ARTICLE II
Section 1.

The Executive power shall be vested in a President of the United States of America. He shall hold his office during the term of four years, and, together with the Vice President, chosen for the same term, be elected, as follows:

Each state shall appoint, in such manner as the Legislature thereof may direct, a number of electors, equal to the whole number of Senators and Representatives to which the State may be entitled in the Congress: but no Senator or Representative, or person holding an office of trust or profit under the United States, shall be appointed an elector.

The electors shall meet in their respective States, and vote by ballot for two persons, of whom one at least shall not be an inhabitant of the Same state with themselves. And they shall make a list of all the persons voted for, and of the number of votes for each; which list they shall sign and certify, and transmit sealed to the seat of the Government of the United States, directed to the President of the Senate. The President of the Senate shall, in the presence of the Senate and House of Representatives, open all the certificates, and the votes shall then be counted. The person having the greatest number of votes shall be the President, if such number be a majority of the whole number of electors appointed; and if there be more than one who have such majority, and have an equal number of votes, then the House of Representatives shall immediately choose by ballot one of them for President; and if no person have a majority, then from the five highest on the list the said House shall in like manner choose the President. But in choosing the President, the votes shall be taken by States, the representation from each state having one vote; A quorum for this purpose shall consist of a member or members from two thirds of the States, and a majority of all the States shall be necessary to a choice. In every case, after the choice of the President, the person having the greatest number of votes of the electors shall be the Vice President. But if there should remain two or more who have equal votes, the Senate shall choose from them by ballot the Vice President.

The Congress may determine the time of choosing the electors, and the day on which they shall give their votes; which day shall be the same throughout the United States.

No person except a natural born citizen, or a citizen of the United States, at the time of the adoption of this Constitution, shall be eligible to the office of President; neither shall any person be eligible to that office who shall not have attained to the age of thirty five years, and been fourteen Years a resident within the United States.

In case of the removal of the President from office, or of his death, resignation, or inability to discharge the powers and duties of the said office, the same shall devolve on the Vice President, and the Congress may by law provide for the case of removal, death, resignation or inability, both of the President and Vice President, declaring what officer shall then act as President, and such officer shall act accordingly, until the disability be removed, or a President shall be elected.

The President shall, at stated times, receive for his services, a compensation, which shall neither be increased nor diminished during the period for which he shall have been elected, and he shall not receive within that period any other emolument from the United States, or any of them.

Before he enter on the execution of his office, he shall take the following oath or affirmation:—"I do solemnly swear (or affirm) that I will faithfully execute the office of President of the United States, and will to the best of my ability, preserve, protect and defend the Constitution of the United States."

Section 2.

The President shall be Commander in Chief of the Army and Navy of the United States, and of the militia of the several States, when called into the actual service of the United States; he may require the opinion, in writing, of the principal officer in each of the executive departments, upon any subject relating to the duties of their respective offices, and he shall have power to grant reprieves and pardons for offenses against the United States, except in cases of impeachment.

He shall have power, by and with the advice and consent of the Senate, to make treaties, provided two thirds of the Senators present concur; and he shall nominate, and by and with the advice and consent of the Senate, shall appoint ambassadors, other public ministers and consuls, judges of the Supreme Court, and all other officers of the United States, whose appointments are not herein otherwise provided for, and which shall be established by law: but the Congress may by law vest the appointment of such inferior officers, as they think proper, in the President alone, in the courts of law, or in the heads of departments.

The President shall have power to fill up all vacancies that may happen during the recess of the Senate, by granting commissions which shall expire at the end of their next session.

Section 3.
He shall from time to time give to the Congress information of the state of the Union, and recommend to their consideration such measures as he shall judge necessary and expedient; he may, on extraordinary occasions, convene both Houses, or either of them, and in case of disagreement between them, with respect to the time of adjournment, he may adjourn them to such time as he shall think proper; he shall receive ambassadors and other public ministers; he shall take care that the laws be faithfully executed, and shall commission all the officers of the United States.

Section 4.
The President, Vice President and all civil officers of the United States, shall be removed from office on impeachment for, and conviction of, treason, bribery, or other high crimes and misdemeanors.

ARTICLE III
Section 1.
The judicial power of the United States, shall be vested in one supreme court, and in such inferior courts as the Congress may from time to time ordain and establish. The judges, both of the supreme and inferior courts, shall hold their offices during good behaviour, and shall, at stated times, receive for their services a compensation, which shall not be diminished during their continuance in office.

Section 2.
The judicial power shall extend to all cases, in law and equity, arising under this constitution, the laws of the United States, and treaties made, or which shall be made, under their authority;—to all cases affecting ambassadors, other public ministers and consuls;—to all cases of admiralty and maritime jurisdiction;—to controversies to which the United States shall be a party;—to controversies between two or more states;—between a state and citizens of another state;—between citizens of different states;—between citizens of the same state claiming lands under grants of different states, and between a state, or the citizens thereof, and foreign states, citizens or subjects.

In all cases affecting ambassadors, other public ministers and consuls, and those in which a state shall be party, the supreme court shall have original jurisdiction. In all the other cases before mentioned, the supreme court shall have appellate jurisdiction, both as to law and fact, with such exceptions, and under such regulations as the Congress shall make.

The trial of all crimes, except in cases of impeachment, shall be by jury; and such trial shall be held in the state where the said crimes shall have been committed; but when not committed within any state, the trial shall be at such place or places as the Congress may by law have directed.

Section 3.
Treason against the United States, shall consist only in levying war against them, or in adhering to their enemies, giving them aid and comfort. No person shall be convicted of treason unless on the testimony of two witnesses to the same overt act, or on confession in open court.

The Congress shall have power to declare the punishment of treason, but no attainder of treason shall work corruption of blood, or forfeiture except during the life of the person attainted.

ARTICLE IV
Section 1.
Full faith and credit shall be given in each state to the public acts, records and judicial proceedings of every other state. And the Congress may by general laws prescribe the manner in which such acts, records, and proceedings shall be proved, and the effect thereof.

Section 2.
The citizens of each state shall be entitled to all privileges and immunities of citizens in the several states.

A person charged in any state with treason, felony, or other crime, who shall flee from justice, and be found in another state, shall on demand of the executive authority of the state from which he fled, be delivered up, to be removed to the state having jurisdiction of the crime.

No person held to service or labor in one state, under the laws thereof, escaping into another, shall, in consequence of any law or regulation therein, be discharged from such service or labor, but shall be delivered up on claim of the party to whom such service or labor may be due.

Section 3.
New states may be admitted by the Congress into this union; but no new state shall be formed or erected within the jurisdiction of any other state; nor any state be formed by the junction of two or more states, or parts of states, without the consent of the Legislatures of the states concerned as well as of the Congress.

The Congress shall have power to dispose of and make all needful rules and regulations respecting the territory or other property belonging to the United States; and nothing in this constitution shall be so construed as to prejudice any claims of the United States, or of any particular state.

Section 4.
The United States shall guarantee to every state in this union a republican form of government, and shall protect each of them against invasion; and on application of the Legislature, or of the executive (when the Legislature cannot be convened), against domestic violence.

ARTICLE V
The Congress, whenever two thirds of both houses shall deem it necessary, shall propose amendments to this constitution, or, on the application of the Legislatures of two thirds of the several states, shall call a convention for proposing amendments, which, in either case, shall be valid to all intents and purposes, as part of this constitution, when ratified by the Legislatures of three fourths of the several states, or by conventions in three fourths thereof, as the one or the other mode of ratification may be proposed by the Congress; Provided that no amendment which may be made prior to the year one thousand eight hundred and eight shall in any manner affect the first and fourth clauses in the ninth section of the first article; and that no state, without its consent, shall be deprived of its equal suffrage in the Senate.

ARTICLE VI

All debts contracted and engagements entered into, before the adoption of this constitution, shall be as valid against the United States under this constitution, as under the confederation.

This constitution, and the laws of the United States which shall be made in pursuance thereof; and all treaties made, or which shall be made, under the authority of the United States, shall be the supreme law of the land; and the judges in every state shall be bound thereby, anything in the constitution or laws of any state to the contrary notwithstanding.

The senators and representatives before mentioned, and the members of the several state Legislatures, and all executive and judicial officers, both of the United States and of the several states, shall be bound by oath or affirmation, to support this constitution; but no religious test shall ever be required as a qualification to any office or public trust under the United States.

ARTICLE VII

The ratification of the conventions of nine states, shall be sufficient for the establishment of this constitution between the states so ratifying the same.

Done in convention by the unanimous consent of the states present the seventeenth day of September in the year of our Lord one thousand seven hundred and eighty seven and of the independence of the United States of America the twelfth. In witness whereof We have hereunto subscribed our Names,

G. Washington—Presid.
and deputy from Virginia

New Hampshire	*Massachusetts*
John Langdon	Nathaniel Gorham
Nicholas Gilman	Rufus King
Connecticut	*New York*
Wm. Saml. Johnson	Alexander Hamilton
Roger Sherman	

New Jersey
Wil: Livingston
David Brearley
Wm. Paterson
Jona: Dayton

Pennsylvania
B Franklin
Thomas Mifflin
Robt Morris
Geo. Clymer
Thos. FitzSimons
Jared Ingersoll
James Wilson
Gouv Morris

Delaware
Geo: Read
Gunning Bedford jun
John Dickinson
Richard Bassett
Jaco: Broom

Maryland
James McHenry
Dan of St Thos. Jenifer
Danl Carroll

Virginia
John Blair—
James Madison Jr.

North Carolina
Wm. Blount
Richd. Dobbs Spaight
Hu Williamson

South Carolina
J. Rutledge
Charles Cotesworth Pinckney
Charles Pinckney
Pierce Butler

Georgia
William Few
Abr Baldwin

Amendments to the Constitution of the United States

AMENDMENT I (1791)
Congress shall make no law respecting an establishment of religion, or prohibiting the free exercise thereof; or abridging the freedom of speech, or of the press; or the right of the people peaceably to assemble, and to petition the Government for a redress of grievances.

AMENDMENT II (1791)
A well regulated militia, being necessary to the security of a free State, the right of the people to keep and bear arms, shall not be infringed.

AMENDMENT III (1791)
No soldier shall, in time of peace be quartered in any house, without the consent of the owner, nor in time of war, but in a manner to be prescribed by law.

AMENDMENT IV (1791)
The right of the people to be secure in their persons, houses, papers, and effects, against unreasonable searches and seizures, shall not be violated, and no warrants shall issue, but upon probable cause, supported by oath or affirmation, and particularly describing the place to be searched, and the persons or things to be seized.

AMENDMENT V (1791)
No person shall be held to answer for a capital, or otherwise infamous crime, unless on a presentment or indictment of a Grand Jury, except in cases arising in the land or naval forces, or in the militia, when in actual service in time of war or public danger; nor shall any person be subject for the same offense to be twice put in jeopardy of life or limb; nor shall be compelled in any criminal case to be a witness against himself, nor be deprived of life, liberty, or property, without due process of law; nor shall private property be taken for public use, without just compensation.

AMENDMENT VI (1791)

In all criminal prosecutions, the accused shall enjoy the right to a speedy and public trial, by an impartial jury of the State and district wherein the crime shall have been committed, which district shall have been previously ascertained by law, and to be informed of the nature and cause of the accusation; to be confronted with the witnesses against him; to have compulsory process for obtaining witnesses in his favor, and to have the assistance of counsel for his defense.

AMENDMENT VII (1791)

In suits at common law, where the value in controversy shall exceed twenty dollars, the right of trial by jury shall be preserved, and no fact tried by a jury, shall be otherwise reexamined in any court of the United States, than according to the rules of the common law.

AMENDMENT VIII (1791)

Excessive bail shall not be required, nor excessive fines imposed, nor cruel and unusual punishments inflicted.

AMENDMENT IX (1791)

The enumeration in the Constitution, of certain rights, shall not be construed to deny or disparage others retained by the people.

AMENDMENT X (1791)

The powers not delegated to the United States by the Constitution, nor prohibited by it to the States, are reserved to the States respectively, or to the people.

AMENDMENT XI (1798)

The judicial power of the United States shall not be construed to extend to any suit in law or equity, commenced or prosecuted against one of the United States by citizens of another State, or by citizens or subjects of any foreign state.

AMENDMENT XII (1804)

The Electors shall meet in their respective States and vote by ballot for President and Vice-President, one of whom, at least, shall not be an inhabitant of the same State with themselves; they shall name in their ballots the person voted for as President, and in distinct ballots the person voted for as Vice-President, and they shall make distinct lists of all persons voted for as President, and of all persons voted for as Vice-President, and of the number of votes for each, which lists they shall sign and certify, and transmit sealed to the seat of the Government of the United States, directed to the President of the Senate;—the President of the Senate shall, in the presence of the Senate and House of Representatives, open all the certificates and the votes shall then be counted;—The person having the greatest number of votes for President, shall be the President, if such number be a majority of the whole number of Electors appointed; and if no person have such majority, then from the persons having the highest numbers not exceeding three on the list of those voted for as President, the House of Representatives shall choose immediately, by ballot, the President. But in choosing the President, the votes shall be taken by States, the representation from each State having one vote; a quorum for this purpose shall consist of a member or members from two-thirds of the states, and a majority of all the states shall be necessary to a choice. And if the House of Representatives shall not choose a President whenever the right of choice shall devolve upon them, before the fourth day of March next following, then the Vice-President shall act as President, as in the case of the death or other constitutional disability of the President. The person having the greatest number of votes as Vice-President, shall be the Vice-President, if such number be a majority of the whole number of electors appointed, and if no person have a majority, then from the two highest numbers on the list, the Senate shall choose the Vice-President; a quorum for the purpose shall consist of two-thirds of the whole number of Senators, and a majority of the whole number shall be necessary to a choice. But no person constitutionally ineligible to the office of President shall be eligible to that of Vice-President of the United States.

AMENDMENT XIII (1865)
Section 1.
Neither slavery nor involuntary servitude, except as a punishment for crime whereof the party shall have been duly convicted, shall exist within the United States, or any place subject to their jurisdiction.

Section 2.
Congress shall have power to enforce this article by appropriate legislation.

AMENDMENT XIV (1868)
Section 1.
All persons born or naturalized in the United States, and subject to the jurisdiction thereof, are citizens of the United States and of the State wherein they reside. No State shall make or enforce any law which shall abridge the privileges or immunities of citizens of the United States; nor shall any state deprive any person of life, liberty, or property, without due process of law; nor deny to any person within its jurisdiction the equal protection of the laws.

Section 2.
Representatives shall be apportioned among the several states according to their respective numbers, counting the whole number of persons in each State, excluding Indians not taxed. But when the right to vote at any election for the choice of Electors for President and Vice-President of the United States, Representatives in Congress, the executive and judicial officers of a State, or the members of the Legislature thereof, is denied to any of the male inhabitants of such State, being twenty-one years of age, and citizens of the United States, or in any way abridged, except for participation in rebellion, or other crime, the basis of representation therein shall be reduced in the proportion which the number of such male citizens shall bear to the whole number of male citizens twenty-one years of age in such State.

Section 3.
No person shall be a Senator or Representative in Congress, or Elector of President and Vice-President, or hold any office, civil or military, under the United States, or under any State, who, having previously taken an oath, as a member of Congress, or as an officer of the United States, or as a member of any State Legislature, or as an executive or judicial officer of any State, to support the Constitution of the United States, shall have engaged in insurrection or rebellion against the same, or given aid or comfort to the enemies thereof. But Congress may by a vote of two-thirds of each House, remove such disability.

Section 4.
The validity of the public debt of the United States, authorized by law, including debts incurred for payment of pensions and bounties for services in suppressing insurrection or rebellion, shall not be questioned. But neither the United States nor any state shall assume or pay any debt or obligation incurred in aid of insurrection or rebellion against the United States, or any claim for the loss or emancipation of any slave; but all such debts, obligations and claims shall be held illegal and void.

Section 5.
The Congress shall have power to enforce, by appropriate legislation, the provisions of this article.

AMENDMENT XV (1870)
Section 1.
The right of citizens of the United States to vote shall not be denied or abridged by the United States or by any State on account of race, color, or previous condition of servitude.

Section 2.
The Congress shall have power to enforce this article by appropriate legislation.

AMENDMENT XVI (1913)
The Congress shall have power to lay and collect taxes on incomes, from whatever source derived, without apportionment among the several States, and without regard to any census or enumeration.

AMENDMENT XVII (1913)
The Senate of the United States shall be composed of two Senators from each State, elected by the people thereof, for six years; and each Senator shall have one vote. The electors in each State shall have the qualifications requisite for electors of the most numerous branch of the State Legislatures.

When vacancies happen in the representation of any State in the Senate, the executive authority of such State shall issue writs of election to fill such vacancies: Provided, That the Legislature of any State may empower the Executive thereof to make temporary appointments until the people fill the vacancies by election as the Legislature may direct.

This amendment shall not be so construed as to affect the election or term of any Senator chosen before it becomes valid as part of the Constitution.

AMENDMENT XVIII (1919)
Section 1.
After one year from the ratification of this article the manufacture, sale, or transportation of intoxicating liquors within, the importation thereof into, or the exportation thereof from the United States and all territory subject to the jurisdiction thereof for beverage purposes is hereby prohibited.

Section 2.
The Congress and the several States shall have concurrent power to enforce this article by appropriate legislation.

Section 3.
This article shall be inoperative unless it shall have been ratified as an amendment to the Constitution by the Legislatures of the several States, as provided in the Constitution, within seven years from the date of the submission hereof to the States by the Congress.

AMENDMENT XIX (1920)
The right of citizens of the United States to vote shall not be denied or abridged by the United States or by any State on account of sex.

Congress shall have power to enforce this article by appropriate legislation.

AMENDMENT XX (1933)
Section 1.
The terms of the President and the Vice President shall end at noon on the 20th day of January, and the terms of Senators and Representatives at noon on the 3rd day of January, of the years in which such terms would have ended if this article had not been ratified; and the terms of their successors shall then begin.

Section 2.
The Congress shall assemble at least once in every year, and such meeting shall begin at noon on the 3rd day of January, unless they shall by law appoint a different day.

Section 3.
If, at the time fixed for the beginning of the term of the President, the President elect shall have died, the Vice President elect shall become President. If a President shall not have been chosen before the time fixed for the beginning of his term, or if the President elect shall have failed to qualify, then the Vice President elect shall act as President until a President shall have qualified; and the Congress may by law provide for the case wherein neither a President elect nor a Vice President shall have qualified, declaring who shall then act as President, or the manner in which one who is to act shall be selected, and such person shall act accordingly until a President or Vice President shall have qualified.

Section 4.
The Congress may by law provide for the case of the death of any of the persons from whom the House of Representatives may choose a President whenever the right of choice shall have devolved upon them, and for the case of the death of any of the persons from whom the Senate may choose a Vice President whenever the right of choice shall have devolved upon them.

Section 5.
Sections 1 and 2 shall take effect on the 15th day of October following the ratification of this article.

Section 6.
This article shall be inoperative unless it shall have been ratified as an amendment to the Constitution by the Legislatures of three-fourths of the several States within seven years from the date of its submission.

AMENDMENT XXI (1933)
Section 1.
The Eighteenth article of amendment to the Constitution of the United States is hereby repealed.

Section 2.
The transportation or importation into any State, Territory, or Possession of the United States for delivery or use therein of intoxicating liquors, in violation of the laws thereof, is hereby prohibited.

Section 3.
This article shall be inoperative unless it shall have been ratified as an amendment to the Constitution by conventions in the several States, as provided in the Constitution, within seven years from the date of the submission hereof to the States by the Congress.

AMENDMENT XXII (1951)
Section 1.
No person shall be elected to the office of the President more than twice, and no person who has held the office of President, or acted as President, for more than two years of a term to which some other person was elected President shall be elected to the office of the President more than once. But this Article shall not apply to any person holding the office of President when this Article was proposed by the Congress, and shall not prevent any person who may be holding the office of President, or acting as President, during the term within which this Article becomes operative from holding the office of President or acting as President during the remainder of such term.

Section 2.
This article shall be inoperative unless it shall have been ratified as an amendment to the Constitution by the Legislatures of three-fourths of the several States within seven years from the date of its submission to the States by the Congress.

AMENDMENT XXIII (1961)
Section 1.
The District constituting the seat of Government of the United States shall appoint in such manner as the Congress may direct:

A number of electors of President and Vice President equal to the whole number of Senators and Representatives in Congress to which the District would be entitled if it were a State, but in no event more than the least populous State; they shall be in addition to those appointed by the States, but they shall be considered, for the purposes of the election of President and Vice President, to be electors appointed by a State; and they shall meet in the District and perform such duties as provided by the twelfth article of amendment.

Section 2.
The Congress shall have power to enforce this article by appropriate legislation.

AMENDMENT XXIV (1964)
Section 1.
The right of citizens of the United States to vote in any primary or other election for President or Vice President, for electors for President or Vice President, or for Senator or Representative in Congress, shall not be denied or abridged by the United States or any State by reason of failure to pay any poll tax or other tax.

Section 2.
The Congress shall have power to enforce this article by appropriate legislation.

AMENDMENT XXV (1967)
Section 1.
In case of the removal of the President from office or of his death or resignation, the Vice President shall become President.

Section 2.
Whenever there is a vacancy in the office of the Vice President, the President shall nominate a Vice President who shall take office upon confirmation by a majority vote of both houses of Congress.

Section 3.
Whenever the President transmits to the President pro tempore of the Senate and the Speaker of the House of Representatives his written declaration that he is unable to discharge the powers and duties of his office, and until he transmits to them a written declaration to the contrary, such powers and duties shall be discharged by the Vice President as Acting President.

Section 4.
Whenever the Vice President and a majority of either the principal officers of the executive departments or of such other body as Congress may by law provide, transmit to the President pro tempore of the Senate and the Speaker of the House of Representatives their written declaration that the President is unable to discharge the powers and duties of his office, the Vice President shall immediately assume the powers and duties of the office as Acting President.

Thereafter, when the President transmits to the President pro tempore of the Senate and the Speaker of the House of Representatives his written declaration that no inability exists, he shall resume the powers and duties of his office unless the Vice President and a majority of either the principal officers of the executive department or of such other body as Congress may by law provide, transmit within four days to the President pro tempore of the Senate and the Speaker of the House of Representatives their written declaration that the President is unable to discharge the powers and duties of his office. Thereupon Congress shall decide the issue, assembling within forty-eight hours for that purpose if not in session. If the Congress, within twenty-one days after receipt of the latter written declaration, or, if Congress is not in session, within twenty-one days after Congress is required to assemble, determines by two-thirds vote of both Houses that the President is unable to discharge the powers and duties of his office, the Vice President shall continue to discharge the same as Acting President; otherwise, the President shall resume the powers and duties of his office.

AMENDMENT XXVI (1971)
Section 1.
The right of citizens of the United States, who are 18 years of age or older, to vote shall not be denied or abridged by the United States or any state on account of age.

Section 2.
The Congress shall have power to enforce this article by appropriate legislation.

AMENDMENT XXVII (1992)
No law varying the compensation for the services of the Senators and Representatives shall take effect until an election of Representatives shall have intervened.

The Declaration of Independence

In CONGRESS, July 4, 1776

The unanimous Declaration of the thirteen united States of America,

When in the Course of human events, it becomes necessary for one people to dissolve the political bands which have connected them with another, and to assume among the powers of the earth, the separate and equal station to which the Laws of Nature and of Nature's God entitle them, a decent respect to the opinions of mankind requires that they should declare the causes which impel them to the separation.

We hold these truths to be self-evident, that all men are created equal, that they are endowed by their Creator with certain unalienable Rights, that among these are Life, Liberty and the pursuit of Happiness. —That to secure these rights, Governments are instituted among Men, deriving their just powers from the consent of the governed, —That whenever any Form of Government becomes destructive of these ends, it is the Right of the People to alter or to abolish it, and to institute new Government, laying its foundation on such principles and organizing its powers in such form, as to them shall seem most likely to effect their Safety and Happiness. Prudence, indeed, will dictate that Governments long established should not be changed for light and transient causes; and accordingly all experience hath shewn, that mankind are more disposed to suffer, while evils are sufferable, than to right themselves by abolishing the forms to which they are accustomed. But when a long train of abuses and usurpations, pursuing invariably the same Object evinces a design to reduce them under absolute Despotism, it is their right, it is their duty, to throw off such Government, and to provide new Guards for their future security. —Such has been the patient sufferance of these Colonies; and such is now the necessity which constrains them to alter their former Systems of Government. The history of the present King of Great Britain [George

III] is a history of repeated injuries and usurpations, all having in direct object the establishment of an absolute Tyranny over these States. To prove this, let Facts be submitted to a candid world.

He has refused his Assent to Laws, the most wholesome and necessary for the public good.

He has forbidden his Governors to pass Laws of immediate and pressing importance, unless suspended in their operation till his Assent should be obtained; and when so suspended, he has utterly neglected to attend to them.

He has refused to pass other Laws for the accommodation of large districts of people, unless those people would relinquish the right of Representation in the Legislature, a right inestimable to them and formidable to tyrants only.

He has called together legislative bodies at places unusual, uncomfortable, and distant from the depository of their public Records, for the sole purpose of fatiguing them into compliance with his measures.

He has dissolved Representative Houses repeatedly, for opposing with manly firmness his invasions on the rights of the people.

He has refused for a long time, after such dissolutions, to cause others to be elected; whereby the Legislative powers, incapable of Annihilation, have returned to the People at large for their exercise; the State remaining in the mean time exposed to all the dangers of invasion from without, and convulsions within.

He has endeavoured to prevent the population of these States; for that purpose obstructing the Laws for Naturalization of Foreigners; refusing to pass others to encourage their migrations hither, and raising the conditions of new Appropriations of Lands.

He has obstructed the Administration of Justice, by refusing his Assent to Laws for establishing Judiciary powers.

He has made Judges dependent on his Will alone, for the tenure of their offices, and the amount and payment of their salaries.

He has erected a multitude of New Offices, and sent hither swarms of Officers to harass our people, and eat out their substance.

He has kept among us, in times of peace, Standing Armies without the consent of our Legislatures.

He has affected to render the Military independent of and superior to the Civil power.

He has combined with others to subject us to a jurisdiction foreign to our constitution, and unacknowledged by our laws; giving his Assent to their Acts of pretended Legislation:

For Quartering large bodies of armed troops among us:

For protecting them, by a mock Trial, from punishment for any Murders which they should commit on the Inhabitants of these States:

For cutting off our Trade with all parts of the world:

For imposing Taxes on us without our Consent:

For depriving us in many cases, of the benefits of Trial by Jury:

For transporting us beyond Seas to be tried for pretended offences:

For abolishing the free System of English Laws in a neighbouring Province, establishing therein an Arbitrary government, and enlarging its Boundaries so as to render it at once an example and fit instrument for introducing the same absolute rule into these Colonies:

For taking away our Charters, abolishing our most valuable Laws, and altering fundamentally the Forms of our Governments:

For suspending our own Legislatures, and declaring themselves invested with power to legislate for us in all cases whatsoever.

He has abdicated Government here, by declaring us out of his Protection and waging War against us.

He has plundered our seas, ravaged our Coasts, burnt our towns, and destroyed the lives of our people.

He is at this time transporting large Armies of foreign Mercenaries to compleat the works of death, desolation and tyranny, already begun with circumstances of Cruelty and perfidy scarcely paralleled in the most barbarous ages, and totally unworthy the Head of a civilized nation.

He has constrained our fellow Citizens taken Captive on the high Seas to bear Arms against their Country, to become the executioners of their friends and Brethren, or to fall themselves by their Hands.

He has excited domestic insurrections amongst us, and has endeavoured to bring on the inhabitants of our frontiers, the merciless Indian Savages, whose known rule of warfare, is an undistinguished destruction of all ages, sexes and conditions.

In every stage of these Oppressions We have Petitioned for Redress in the most humble terms: Our repeated Petitions have been answered only by repeated injury. A Prince whose character is thus marked by every act which may define a Tyrant, is unfit to be the ruler of a free people.

Nor have We been wanting in attentions to our British brethren. We have warned them from time to time of attempts by their Legislature to extend an unwarrantable jurisdiction over us. We have reminded them of the circumstances of our emigration and settlement here. We have appealed to their native justice and magnanimity, and we have conjured them by the ties of our common kindred to disavow these usurpations, which, would inevitably interrupt our connections and correspondence. They too have been deaf to the voice of justice and of consanguinity. We must, therefore, acquiesce in the necessity, which denounces our Separation, and hold them, as we hold the rest of mankind, Enemies in War, in Peace Friends.

We, therefore, the Representatives of the united States of America, in General Congress, Assembled, appealing to the Supreme Judge of the world for the rectitude of our intentions, do, in the Name, and by the Authority of the good People of these Colonies, solemnly publish and declare, That these United Colonies are, and of Right ought to be Free and Independent States; that they are Absolved from all Allegiance to the British Crown, and that all political connection between them and the State of Great Britain, is and ought to be totally dissolved; and that as Free and Independent States, they have full Power to levy War, conclude Peace, contract Alliances, establish Commerce, and to do all other Acts and Things which Independent States may of right do. And for the support of this Declaration, with a firm reliance on the protection of divine Providence, we mutually pledge to each other our Lives, our Fortunes and our sacred Honor.

The signers of the Declaration represented the new states as follows:

New Hampshire
Josiah Bartlett
William Whipple
Matthew Thornton

Massachusetts
John Hancock
Samual Adams
John Adams
Robert Treat Paine
Elbridge Gerry

Rhode Island
Stephen Hopkins
William Ellery

Connecticut
Roger Sherman
Samuel Huntington
William Williams
Oliver Wolcott

New York
William Floyd
Philip Livingston
Francis Lewis
Lewis Morris

New Jersey
Richard Stockton
John Witherspoon
Francis Hopkinson
John Hart
Abraham Clark

Pennsylvania
Robert Morris
Benjamin Rush
Benjamin Franklin
John Morton
George Clymer
James Smith
George Taylor
James Wilson
George Ross

Delaware
Caesar Rodney
George Read
Thomas McKean

Maryland
Samuel Chase
William Paca
Thomas Stone
Charles Carroll of Carrollton

Virginia
George Wythe
Richard Henry Lee
Thomas Jefferson
Benjamin Harrison
Thomas Nelson, Jr.
Francis Lightfoot Lee
Carter Braxton

North Carolina
William Hooper
Joseph Hewes
John Penn

South Carolina
Edward Rutledge
Thomas Heyward, Jr.
Thomas Lynch, Jr.
Arthur Middleton

Georgia
Button Gwinnett
Lyman Hall
George Walton

Notes

1. Central Intelligence Agency, "The World Factbook: Rank Order—Population," http://www.cia.gov/cia/publications/factbook/rankorder/2119rank.html.
2. Andrew Martin and Andrew Zajac, "Flood Control Funds Short of Requests," *Chicago Tribune*, September 1, 2005.
3. Ace Project, "Swiss Direct Democracy," Ace Focus on Direct Democracy, http://focus.aceproject.org/direct-democracy/cs-swiss.
4. Mothers Against Drunk Driving, "Statistics," http://www.madd.org/stats/1112.
5. Ibid.
6. Centers for Disease Control and Prevention, "Annual Smoking-Attributable Mortality, Years of Potential Life Lost, and Economic Costs: United States, 1995–1999," *Morbidity and Mortality Weekly Report*, April 12, 2002, http://www.cdc.gov/mmwr/preview/mmwrhtml/mm5114a2.htm.
7. Death Penalty Information Center, "Facts about Deterrence and the Death Penalty," http://www.deathpenaltyinfo.org/article.php?scid=12&did=167.
8. Centers for Disease Control and Prevention, *National Vital Statistics Report 53*, no. 5 (October 12, 2004).
9. Ibid.
10. Reference.com, s.v. "Pornography," http://www.reference.com/browse/wiki/Pornography.
11. Marianne Szegedy-Maszak, "Ensnared," *Los Angeles Times*, December 26, 2005.
12. Interpol, "Legislation of Interpol Member States on Sexual Offences against Children: Netherlands," http://www.interpol.int/Public/Children/SexualAbuse/NationalLaws/csaNetherlands.asp.
13. Bureau of Democracy, Human Rights, and Labor, "The Netherlands: Country Reports on Human Rights Practices," February 25, 2004, U.S. Department of State, http://www.state.gov/g/drl/rls/hrrpt/2003/27856.htm.

14. Kit R. Roane, "World's Oldest Profession Moves Off the Streets," *New York Times,* February 23, 1998, Factbook on Global Sexual Exploitation, http://www.uri.edu/artsci/wms/hughes/factbook.htm.
15. Wikipedia, s.v. "Publicly-funded Medicine," http://en.wikipedia.org/wiki/Publicly_funded_medicine.
16. Liz Pulliam Weston, "Big Medical Bills Sometimes Make Bankruptcy Necessary," *Los Angeles Times,* July 24, 2005.
17. Alicia Chang, "Drug Companies Influence Medical Research," NBC Health News, May 25, 2005. Chang notes that private industry funds more than two-thirds of the medical research done at U.S. universities.
18. Wikipedia, s.v. "United States Presidential Election, 2000," http://en.wikipedia.org/wiki/U.S._presidential_election_2000.
19. Texas State Library & Archives Commission, "Annexation Process: 1836–1845—A Summary Timeline," http://www.tsl.state.tx.us/ref/abouttx/annexation/timeline.html. Snopes.com maintains that a two-vote difference led to formal annexation, followed by ratification by the Texas Congress and voters. For this and other one-vote fallacies and the reasons they persist, see http://www.snopes.com/history/govern/onevote.htm.
20. Snopes.com, "'One Vote' Fallacies," http://www.snopes.com/history/govern/onevote.htm.
21. Wendy Koch, "'Go-getter,' 18, Ousts Mayor in Michigan," *USA Today,* November 9, 2005.
22. Alaska Division of Elections, "Your Vote Counts," http://www.ltgov.state.ak.us/ltgov/elections/votecnts.htm.
23. Ibid.
24. Iowa Official Register, "Voter Registration," http://www.sos.state.ia.us/elections/voterreg/.
25. National Court Reporters Association, "Grass Roots Lobbying," http://www.ncraonline.org/ppa/grassroots/vote.shtml.
26. Ibid.
27. U.S. House of Representatives, Office of the Clerk, http://clerk.house.gov/evs/2003/roll444.xml.
28. Calvin R. Trice, "Here's Proof Each Vote Counts," *Richmond Times-Dispatch,* November 10, 2005.

29. League of Women Voters of Massachusetts, "Your Vote Makes a Difference," http://www.ma.lwv.org/ElectionPubs/your_vote.htm.
30. Seth Mandel, "Farkas Wins Council Seat—By One Vote," *East Brunswick Sentinel*, November 23, 2005.
31. Seth Mandel, "Election Tally Reverses; Cruz Wins by One Vote," *East Brunswick Sentinel*, December 1, 2005.
32. National Women's History Project, "Proclamation Sample," http://www.nwhp.org/events/anniversary/85th-celebration/proclamation-sample.html.

Index

abortion, 7
affirmative action, 9
Allen, James C., 67
amendments to the Constitution.
 See United States Constitution
antiterrorism, 57

Balderston, Karen, 67
Bill of Rights, 13
Britain, 59
Burn, Harry, 69
Bush, George W., 1–2, 65
Byrne, Leslie, 68

Call, Larry, 67
capital punishment, 15
children, 23, 29, 47, 49, 51, 69
church and state, separation of, 53
Coleman, Nicholas, 67
Constitution of the United States. *See*
 United States Constitution
Cruz, Joseph, 68–69

Death Penalty Information Center, 15
debt, national, 41
Declaration of Independence (full
 text), 99–104
direct democracy, about, 2, 3
disenfranchisement, 1–2
drafts, military, 33
drinking age, 67
drugs, decriminalization of, 39
Dunn, George G., 67
Durkin, John, 68

education, 51, 68, 69
elections/voting
 close elections, 65–70
 Electoral College, 17
 polling versus, 4
 reasons for not, 1–2

Electoral College, 17
Emond, Robert, 67
English language, 45
entitlements, 19
euthanasia, voluntary, 61
executions, 15

"Facts about Deterrence and the
 Death Penalty," 15
Farkas, Randy, 68–69
federal debt, 41
firearms, banning, 29
Flournoy, Thomas S., 68
foreign aid, 21, 37
foster care, 23
free speech, 25

gambling, 27
gun banning/gun control, 29

Hammond, Jay, 66
Head Start, 68
healthcare, 35, 59, 61
Hellyer, Bob, 67
Hickel, Walter, 66
Hitler, Adolf, 65

identity cards, national, 43
illegal drugs, decriminalization of,
 39
immigration, illegal, 31, 43
Internal Revenue Service, 55

Jefferson, Thomas, 13, 53
Johnson, Andrew, 66
Johnson, Henry S., 66

Katrina, Hurricane, 2
Kelly, Tim, 66
Knowles, Tony, 66
Kreiman, Keith, 67

language, national, 45, 65
Lansing (Michigan) School District, 67
legislation, 4
life imprisonment, 15
Luthi, Randall, 67

Mayo, Robert M., 67
McCormick, Mark, 67
McCracken, David, 66
McIntyre, John, 68
Medicaid, 35
military service, mandatory, 33
military spending, 37
minorities, 9
morality issues, 25
Morton, Marcus "Landslide," 65

narcotics decriminalization, 39
national debt, 41
national identity cards, 43
national language, 45, 65
national security, 57
National Women's History Project, 69
Nixon, Sydney, 67

organized crime, 11

passports, 43
Pfaelzer, Mariana, 1
political system, origin of, 3–5
politicians, 2, 4
pornography, 47
privacy, 43
prohibition
    alcohol and tobacco, 11
    gambling, 27
    narcotics, 39
    pornography, 47
    prostitution, 49
Proposition 187 (California), 1
prostitution, 49
public opinion, 4
public schools financing, 51

Rants, Christopher, 67
Ratcliff, Mary, 66
religious liberty, 53
retirement income, 19
rights, 4
    bearing arms, 29

rights, *continued*
    Bill of Rights, 57
    civil, 43
ruling bodies, 2

schools, financing public, 51
Schuerer, Neal, 67
security, national, 57
separation of church and state, 53
Sessions, Michael, 66
Sherwood, Donald, 68
Social Security, 19
special circumstances punishment
    (for heinous crimes), 15
Spohnholz, Ann, 66
state-level direct democracy, 3
state sanctioning of abortion, 7
Sullivan, Mike, 68
Supreme Court, 1–2, 17
Switzerland, 3, 4

taxation, 55
terrorism, 57
Texas annexation, 66
treason, 15

Uehling, Rick, 66
Ulmer, Fran, 66
United States Constitution
    amending, 13
    First Amendment (free speech),
        25, 47
    full text of, 71–85, 87–97
    Nineteenth Amendment, 69–70
    Second Amendment (right to bear
        arms), 29
    separation of church and state,
        53
universal healthcare, 59

Vezey, Al, 66
Vilsack, Thomas, 67
voluntary euthanasia, 61
voting. *See* elections/voting

wars, spending on, 37
Web sites, 62, 70
welfare income, 19
White House address, 62
Wick, Hal, 68
Wyman, Louis, 68

About the Author

W. R. Wilkerson III is a published author and songwriter. His books include *The Man Who Invented Las Vegas* (Ciro's Books, 2000); *All-American Ads of the 40s*, edited by Jim Heimann, (Taschen, 2002); *Las Vegas Vintage Graphics* (Taschen, 2003); and the upcoming *Paradise* (Ciro's Books, 2007).

Abortion
Should abortion continue to be sanctioned by the state?

YES ○   NO ○

Affirmative Action
Should affirmative action policies, which give preferential treatment based on minority status, be protected?

YES ○   NO ○

Alcohol & Tobacco Prohibition
Should alcohol and tobacco be prohibited?

YES ○   NO ○

Amending the Constitution
Should changes or further amendments to the Constitution of the United States of America be allowed by law?

YES ○   NO ○

Capital Punishment
Should capital punishment be mandated by law?

YES ○   NO ○

Electoral College
Should the Electoral College be retained?

YES ○   NO ○

Entitlements (Social Security & Welfare)
Should entitlements be maintained?

YES ○   NO ○

Foreign Aid
Should foreign aid continue?

YES ○   NO ○

Foster Care
Should the foster care system be maintained?

YES ○   NO ○

Free Speech
Should freedom of speech always be protected?

YES ○   NO ○

Gambling
Should gambling be legalized nationwide?

YES ○   NO ○

Gun Banning
Should guns be banned?

YES ○   NO ○

Illegal Immigration
Should illegal immigration be tolerated?

YES ○   NO ○

Mandatory National Service
Should national service be mandatory?

YES ○   NO ○

Medicaid
Should Medicaid be preserved?

YES ○   NO ○

Military Spending
Should we continue to fund military spending at or above the levels we have funded it for the past fifty years?

YES ○   NO ○

Narcotics Decriminalization
Should narcotics be decriminalized?

YES ○   NO ○

National Debt
Should the national debt be allowed to continue?

YES ○   NO ○

National Identity Card
Should a national identity card be implemented?

YES ○   NO ○

National Language
Should a single national language be instituted?

YES ○   NO ○

Pornography
Should pornography be legal?

YES ○   NO ○

Prostitution
Should prostitution be legal?

YES ○   NO ○

Public School Financing
Should more money be spent on the public school system?

YES ○   NO ○

Separation of Church & State
Should a division be upheld between church and state?

YES ○   NO ○

Taxation
Should the current system of taxation be maintained?

YES ○   NO ○

Terrorism & Anti-terrorist Measures
Should antiterrorist measures be enacted and kept in place for the foreseeable future?

YES ○   NO ○

Universal Healthcare
Should a universal healthcare system for every American be implemented?

YES ○   NO ○

Voluntary Euthanasia
Should voluntary euthanasia be legal?

YES ○   NO ○

How Would You Vote If You Were Allowed To? by W. R. Wilkerson III © 2006

PLACE
FIRST-CLASS
STAMP
HERE

The President of the United States
The White House
1600 Pennsylvania Avenue NW
Washington, DC 20500

Name: _____
Address: _____

Dear Mr. President,
Please review my ballot and then deliver it to the General Accounting Office to be tabulated with the others like it. Whatever the outcome of the vote, we demand that our wishes be enacted into law.